MW01528370

Copyright 2019 © Kai Kaine. All rights reserved.

Printed in the USA
CPSIA information can be obtained
at www.ICGtesting.com
LVHW020938250524
781393LV00033B/1104

9 781704 889108